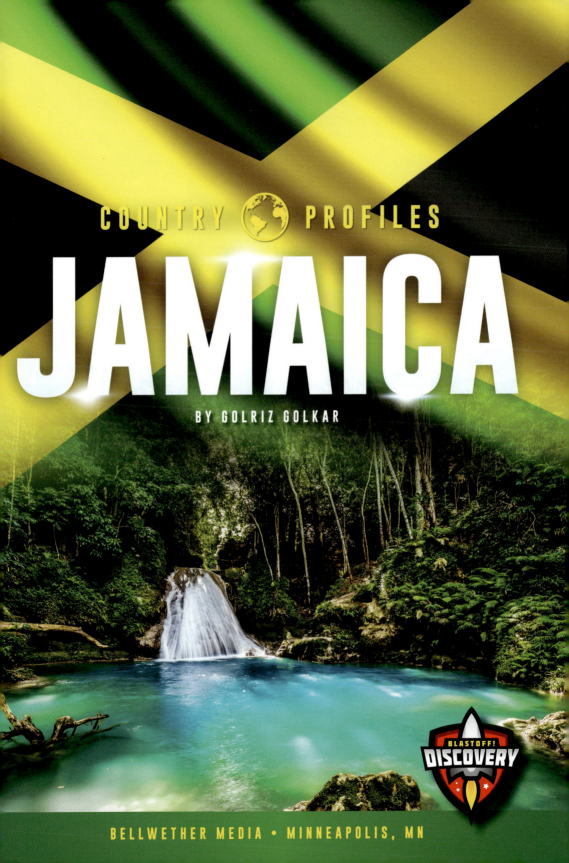

Blastoff! Discovery launches a new mission: reading to learn. Filled with facts and features, each book offers you an exciting new world to explore!

BLASTOFF! UNIVERSE

GRADE K

GRADES 1-3

GRADE 4

This edition first published in 2022 by Bellwether Media, Inc.

No part of this publication may be reproduced in whole or in part without written permission of the publisher.
For information regarding permission, write to Bellwether Media, Inc., Attention: Permissions Department,
6012 Blue Circle Drive, Minnetonka, MN 55343.

Library of Congress Cataloging-in-Publication Data

Names: Golkar, Golriz, author.
Title: Jamaica / by Golriz Golkar.
Description: Minneapolis, MN : Bellwether Media, Inc., 2022. |
Series: Blastoff! discovery: country profiles | Includes bibliographical references and index. | Audience: Ages 7-13 | Audience: Grades 4-6
Summary: "Engaging images accompany information about Jamaica. The combination of high-interest subject matter and narrative text is intended for students in grades 3 through 8." Provided by publisher.
Identifiers: LCCN 2021051737 (print) | LCCN 2021051738 (ebook) | ISBN 9781644876114 (library binding) | ISBN 9781648346224 (ebook)
Subjects: LCSH: Jamaica–Juvenile literature.
Classification: LCC F1868.2 .G65 2022 (print) | LCC F1868.2 (ebook) | DDC 972.92–dc23/eng/20211025
LC record available at https://lccn.loc.gov/2021051737
LC ebook record available at https://lccn.loc.gov/2021051738

Text copyright © 2022 by Bellwether Media, Inc. BLASTOFF! DISCOVERY and associated logos are trademarks and/or registered trademarks of Bellwether Media, Inc.

Editor: Rachael Barnes   Designer: Brittany McIntosh

Printed in the United States of America, North Mankato, MN.

TABLE OF CONTENTS

AN ISLAND PARADISE	4
LOCATION	6
LANDSCAPE AND CLIMATE	8
WILDLIFE	10
PEOPLE	12
COMMUNITIES	14
CUSTOMS	16
SCHOOL AND WORK	18
PLAY	20
FOOD	22
CELEBRATIONS	24
TIMELINE	26
JAMAICA FACTS	28
GLOSSARY	30
TO LEARN MORE	31
INDEX	32

AN ISLAND PARADISE

LIME CAY

A family begins their day in Kingston with a visit to the Tuff Gong recording studio. They learn about the recording process and music of Bob Marley, the famous reggae singer. Next, they take a taxi to the Bob Marley Museum. They see awards and favorite items at the singer's home.

OTHER TOP SITES

BLUE MOUNTAINS

DEVON HOUSE

GREEN GROTTO CAVES

LUMINOUS LAGOON

Afternoon brings a stroll through the Kingston Craft Market. They buy colorful handmade Jamaican hats. Then, the family boats to Lime **Cay** to relax on the beach. They sip refreshing *sorrel* tea while taking in the turquoise waters. Jamaica is a true island paradise!

LOCATION

Jamaica is a small island country located in the Caribbean Sea. It covers 4,244 square miles (10,991 square kilometers). It is part of the **Greater Antilles** island chain northeast of Central America. Cuba is Jamaica's closest neighboring country. It lies north of Jamaica. Haiti is to Jamaica's east. The Cayman Islands sit northwest of Jamaica.

TINY ISLAND

Jamaica is only 51 miles (82 kilometers) wide at its widest point. It takes less than a day to drive around the entire island.

Jamaica's capital, Kingston, is located on the island's southeastern coast. Jamaica has several sandy cays just off the **mainland**. They rest on **coral reefs** and may be visited by boat. The Port Royal Cays are near Kingston Harbor.

7

LANDSCAPE AND CLIMATE

Jamaica is mostly mountainous. **Rain forests** dot the landscape from the western valleys to the eastern mountains. The **terrain** peaks at the Blue Mountains in the east. A large limestone **plateau** stretches across the island. Cliffs and caves break up the plateau. Jamaica's longest river, the Rio Minho, flows south from central Jamaica. White sand beaches line the island's coasts. Coral reefs lie in the coastal waters.

Y.S. FALLS

BLUE MOUNTAINS

KINGSTON
Average seasonal highs and lows

JANUARY
HIGH: 85 °F (29 °C)
LOW: 74 °F (23 °C)

APRIL
HIGH: 87 °F (31 °C)
LOW: 77 °F (25 °C)

JULY
HIGH: 89 °F (32 °C)
LOW: 80 °F (27 °C)

OCTOBER
HIGH: 88 °F (31 °C)
LOW: 78 °F (26 °C)

°F = degrees Fahrenheit
°C = degrees Celsius

Jamaica has a **tropical** climate. Temperatures are warm year-round. Spring and fall are rainy seasons. Mountainous regions receive the most rain, while the southern coast has little rainfall. **Hurricane** season lasts from summer through fall.

WILDLIFE

Jamaica is home to many animals. Mongooses scurry around cities and many parts of the countryside. They feast on snakes, rats, and lizards. At night, Jamaican coneys roam the mountains. Jamaican owls hoot in the surrounding trees. Jamaican fruit bats rest in caves and hollow trees. The red-billed streamertail, the national bird, flies about. **Migrating** falcons fly to the rain forest each winter.

Manatees swim in the coastal waters while munching on seagrass. American crocodiles live in salty waters. They hunt for fish, crabs, and birds. Many leatherback sea turtles and coral reef fish live in protected northern waters.

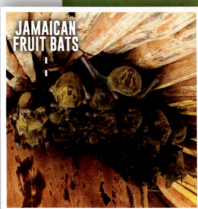

JAMAICAN FRUIT BATS

LEATHERBACK SEA TURTLE

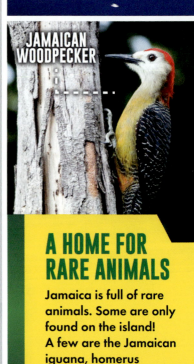

JAMAICAN WOODPECKER

A HOME FOR RARE ANIMALS

Jamaica is full of rare animals. Some are only found on the island! A few are the Jamaican iguana, homerus swallowtail butterfly, and Jamaican woodpecker.

AMERICAN CROCODILE

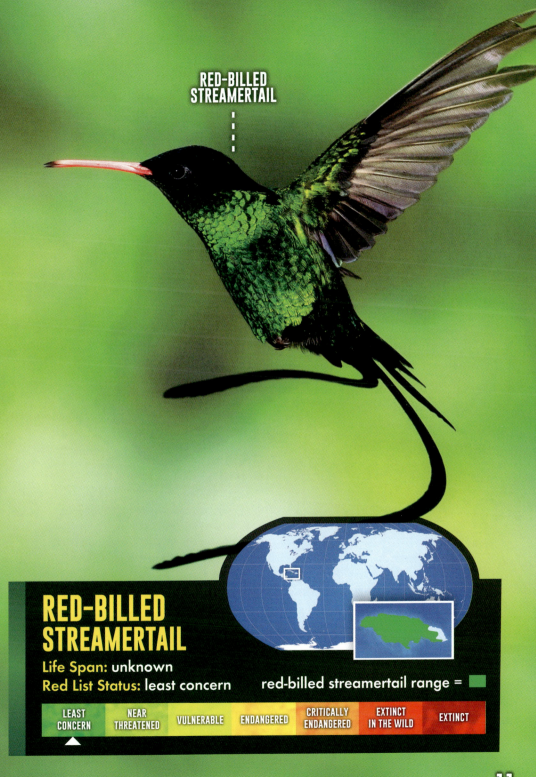

PEOPLE

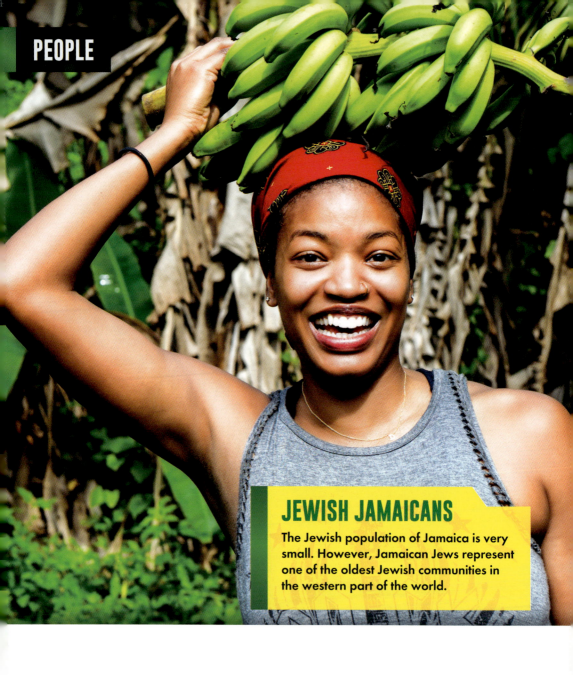

JEWISH JAMAICANS

The Jewish population of Jamaica is very small. However, Jamaican Jews represent one of the oldest Jewish communities in the western part of the world.

Jamaica is home to nearly 3 million people. Around 9 out of 10 Jamaicans have African roots. Others have mixed African and European **ancestry**. A small number of people in Jamaica are from China, India, and Europe. Jamaicans are proud of their **culture** and the saying: "Out of Many, One People."

Most Jamaicans are Protestants. Small groups are Hindu, Muslim, Buddhist, or Jewish. Some Jamaicans are Rastafarians. Their religion combines Christian and African elements. English is the official language of Jamaica. But Jamaicans more often speak Patois. The language combines English with African, Spanish, and some French.

FAMOUS FACE

Name: Usain Bolt
Birthday: August 21, 1986
Hometown: Sherwood Content, Jamaica
Famous for: Eight-time Olympic gold medalist in sprinting, who holds several world records and is considered the greatest sprinter of all time

SPEAK JAMAICAN PATOIS

ENGLISH	JAMAICAN PATOIS	HOW TO SAY IT
hello	wah gwan	WAAH gwon
goodbye	mi gaan	me GAHN
please	a beg yuh	ah beg YUH
thank you	tanks	tanks
yes	yeh	YEH
no	no	nuh

KINGSTON

COMMUNITIES

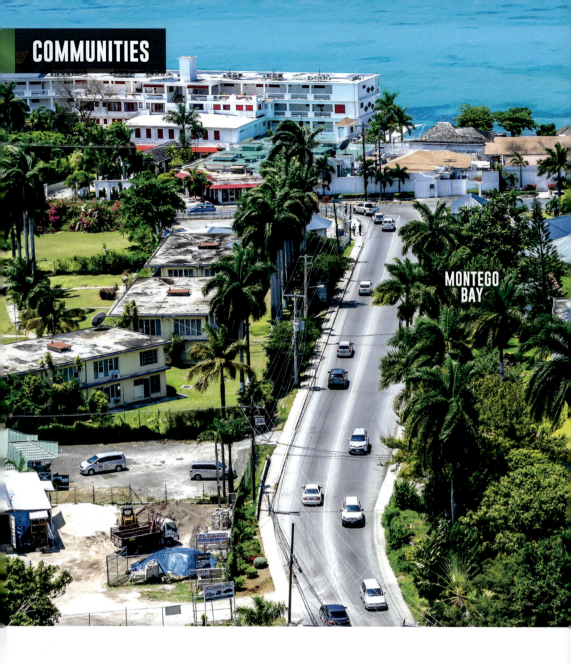

MONTEGO BAY

More than half of all Jamaicans live in **urban** areas. Kingston and other coastal cities are the most populated. People in cities live in small houses or apartment buildings. Cars, buses, and taxis take people around the island. They all drive on the left side of the road.

People in **rural** areas often live in big concrete houses with gardens. They travel by bus or on foot. Some Jamaicans cannot afford sturdy homes. They live in shacks. These homes usually lack electricity or running water.

CUSTOMS

Jamaicans are friendly people. They greet friends and family with a pat on the back or a kiss. They commonly address each other by nicknames. Strangers are greeted with a handshake and addressed by title. Jamaicans enjoy helping family, friends, and neighbors.

THE MUSIC OF BOB MARLEY
Bob Marley is the most famous Jamaican singer and musician. He made Jamaican music and the Patois language known around the world.

REGGAE MUSICIANS

Jamaicans are proud of their musical **heritage**. Reggae is a popular type of music set to drums and guitar. It mixes **traditional** Jamaican musical styles with jazz. Reggae songs share the troubles of mistreated people. Jamaicans also enjoy dancehall. It mixes reggae, rap, and electronic music. Jamaicans also like the steady beat of calypso music played with steel drums.

17

SCHOOL AND WORK

Jamaican children must attend school from ages 7 to 11. Primary education is free. After grade six, students take an exam. Some go on to high school, while others attend trade schools. It is more common for wealthy Jamaicans to study at university.

About 7 out of 10 Jamaicans work in **service jobs**. Many work in Jamaica's **tourism** industry. Others may hold office jobs or work in financial services. Some Jamaicans are agricultural workers. They may care for sugarcane, coffee, or banana crops on **plantations**. Fishing is also an important industry. Some Jamaicans have jobs in mining or construction.

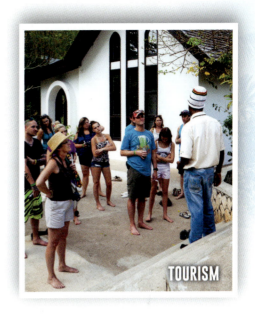

TOURISM

FARMING

PLAY

THE JAMAICAN BOBSLED TEAM

In 1988, the first Jamaican bobsled team competed in the Winter Olympics. While they did not win a medal, their brave story inspired many fans. It also inspired a hit movie called *Cool Runnings*!

JAMAICAN BOBSLED TEAM

Cricket is a favorite sport in Jamaica. It is similar to baseball. Many Jamaican cricket players compete on regional teams. Soccer is also a popular sport to play and watch. Jamaica's national soccer team has played in **World Cup** games. Track and field is another common sport. Jamaica trains and sends many top athletes to world contests, such as the Olympics.

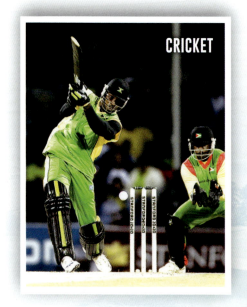

CRICKET

Jamaicans like to play traditional board games and dominoes. They also enjoy the island's natural beauty. Jamaicans often hike, swim, and take vacations on the beach. On weekends, families have a large meal together.

DOMINOES

STUCK AND FREEZE

What You Need:
- A tree or cone to mark a safe zone.

How to Play:
1. Make a catching team and a safe team with equal numbers of players.
2. The teams stand on opposite sides of a field. The safe team starts near the safe zone.
3. After counting to three, the teams run toward each other. The catching team tries to catch the safe team by tapping them.
4. The safe team tries to run back to the safe zone without being tapped. Safe players must run to the catching team's side of the field before running back to the safe zone.
5. If a safe team member is tapped, they freeze in place. They can be "melted" with a tap from another teammate.
6. When a frozen player is melted, both players try to return to the safe zone.
7. If the whole safe team returns to the safe zone without being frozen, they win the round. The teams keep their roles and begin a new round.
8. If the catching team freezes the whole safe team, they win. The teams switch roles and begin a new round.

FOOD

Jamaican food is flavorful. Many Jamaicans eat ackee and saltfish, the national dish, for breakfast. For this meal, salted codfish is eaten with juicy fruits. A soft, thick, boiled meal of spiced corn called porridge is another breakfast favorite. Lunch is usually light. Many Jamaicans pack lunch, or box food, with fish or meat over rice and peas.

Dinner is the main meal. Jamaicans enjoy spicy barbecued *jerk* meats, especially chicken. Goat curries and chicken stews are popular. Salads, plantains, flatbreads, and cooked *callaloo* greens are common side dishes. Tropical fruits and different hot drinks are enjoyed with meals.

ACKEE AND SALTFISH

JERK CHICKEN

JAMAICAN GRATER CAKE

Jamaican grater cake is a sweet and colorful cake that almost tastes like candy. Have an adult help you make it.

Ingredients:
2 1/2 cups dried coconut flakes
1 1/2 cups sugar
1 1/4 cups water
1/4 teaspoon salt
1/4 teaspoon almond extract
red food coloring

Steps:
1. Combine the sugar and water in a pot and bring to a boil.
2. Lower to medium heat. Cook until the mixture is reduced to a thin syrup.
3. Add the coconut, salt, and almond extract to the mixture. Stir until thick.
4. Remove about 1/3 of the mixture and mix it with 1 or 2 drops of red food coloring for a deep pink color. Set it aside.
5. Spread the rest of the coconut mixture evenly in a large, greased casserole dish.
6. Spread the pink coconut mixture thinly over the thicker white layer.
7. Cool for 25 minutes at room temperature. Cut into squares and serve.

CELEBRATIONS

EASTER

Jamaicans celebrate several Christian holidays. They attend church on Good Friday and Easter Sunday. Jamaicans visit friends and family throughout the weekend. They eat traditional fruit and spice buns together. Christmas is also a big celebration. Jamaicans enjoy music, food, and shopping on Christmas Eve. On Christmas Day, families eat a big feast for dinner.

Jamaicans also love national holidays. Spring brings Labor Day. Jamaicans clean and fix up their towns. They volunteer to help people in need. In August, contests, dances, and parades mark Jamaican Independence Day. Jamaicans are proud of their rich culture and history!

INDEPENDENCE DAY

TIMELINE

1509
Spanish colonists occupy Jamaica, bringing African slaves to work on plantations

1655
The British capture Jamaica from Spain

1838
Slavery is officially illegal in Jamaica

1870
Banana plantations are set up as sugar production decreases

1938
Jamaicans riot against unemployment and unfair racial policies, leading to the creation of labor unions and major political parties

1962
Jamaica becomes an independent nation, but still has ties to the United Kingdom

2021
Three Jamaican women win every medal in the 100-meter dash at the Tokyo Summer Olympic Games

1944
A new constitution gives all adults voting rights and the first elections are held for local governments

2016
Jamaica wins 11 medals in the Rio Summer Olympic Games

2006
Portia Simpson Miller becomes Jamaica's first female prime minister

JAMAICA FACTS

Official Name: Jamaica

Flag of Jamaica: A diagonal yellow cross divides the Jamaican flag into four triangles. The top and bottom green triangles represent hope, vegetation, and agriculture. The black triangles to the left and right represent past and future hardships. The yellow cross stands for sunshine and Jamaica's raw materials.

Area: 4,244 square miles (10,991 square kilometers)

Capital City: Kingston

Important Cities: Portmore, Spanish Town, Montego Bay

Population: 2,816,602 (July 2021)

WHERE PEOPLE LIVE

COUNTRYSIDE 43.3%

CITY 56.7%

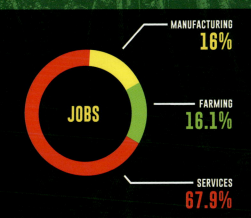

JOBS
- MANUFACTURING **16%**
- FARMING **16.1%**
- SERVICES **67.9%**

Main Exports:

 sugar   bananas   aluminum

 petroleum coffee   bauxite

National Holiday:
Independence Day (August 6)

Main Languages:
English (official), Jamaican Patois

Form of Government:
parliamentary democracy under a constitutional monarchy

Title for Country Leaders:
queen, represented by governor general (chief of state), prime minister (head of government)

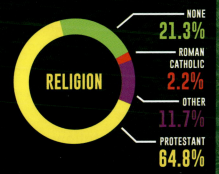

RELIGION
- NONE **21.3%**
- ROMAN CATHOLIC **2.2%**
- OTHER **11.7%**
- PROTESTANT **64.8%**

Unit of Money:
Jamaican dollar

GLOSSARY

ancestry—a person's ancestors; ancestors are relatives who lived long ago.

cay—a small, low island; a cay can also be called a key.

coral reefs—structures made of coral that usually grow in shallow seawater

culture—the beliefs, arts, and ways of life in a place or society

Greater Antilles—a group of four of the largest islands in the Caribbean Sea, including Cuba, Hispaniola, Jamaica, and Puerto Rico

heritage—the traditions, achievements, and beliefs that are part of the history of a group of people

hurricane—related to storms formed in the tropics that have violent winds and often have rain and lightning

mainland—the main part of a country or continent

migrating—traveling from one place to another, often with the seasons

plantations—large farms that grow coffee beans, cotton, rubber, or other crops; plantations are mainly found in warm climates.

plateau—an area of flat, raised land

rain forests—thick, green forests that receive a lot of rain

rural—related to the countryside

service jobs—jobs that perform tasks for people or businesses

terrain—the surface features of an area of land

tourism—the business of people traveling to visit other places

traditional—related to customs, ideas, or beliefs handed down from one generation to the next

tropical—part of the tropics; the tropics is a hot, rainy region near the equator.

urban—related to cities and city life

World Cup—an international soccer competition, held every four years; the World Cup is the world's largest soccer tournament.

TO LEARN MORE

AT THE LIBRARY

Ellison, Katie. *Who Was Bob Marley?* New York, N.Y.: Grosset & Dunlap, 2017.

Levit, Joseph. *Track and Field's G.O.A.T.: Usain Bolt, Jackie Joyner-Kersee, and More.* Minneapolis, Minn.: Lerner Publications, 2022.

Rechner, Amy. *Cuba.* Minneapolis, Minn.: Bellwether Media, 2019.

ON THE WEB

FACTSURFER

Factsurfer.com gives you a safe, fun way to find more information.

1. Go to www.factsurfer.com.

2. Enter "Jamaica" into the search box and click 🔍.

3. Select your book cover to see a list of related content.

INDEX

activities, 21
Bolt, Usain, 13
capital (see Kingston)
celebrations, 24–25
Christmas, 24
climate, 9
communities, 14–15
customs, 16–17
Easter, 24
education, 18
fast facts, 28–29
food, 5, 22–23, 24
housing, 14, 15
Independence Day, 25
Kingston, 4–5, 7, 9, 13, 14
Labor Day, 25
landmarks, 4, 5
landscape, 5, 7, 8–9, 10
language, 13
location, 6–7
Marley, Bob, 4, 16
Montego Bay, 6, 14
music, 4, 16, 17, 24
people, 12–13
Port Royal Cays, 5, 7
recipe, 23
religion, 12, 13
size, 6, 7
sports, 20
stuck and freeze (activity), 21
timeline, 26–27
transportation, 14, 15
wildlife, 10–11
work, 19

The images in this book are reproduced through the courtesy of: PhotoSpirit / Alamy Stock Photo, front cover; Steffan Hill/ Alamy Stock Photo, pp. 4-5; Photo Spirit, p. 5 (Blue Mountains); Mihai-Bogdan Lazar, p. 5 (Devon House); Jason O. Watson/ Alamy Stock Photo, p. 5 (Green Grotto Caves); PhotoSpirit/ Alamy Stock Photo, p. 5 (Luminous Lagoon); AridOcean, pp. 6-7; Sherry Talbot, p. 8; Photo Spirit, p. 9 (Blue Mountains); Carmela Soto, p. 9 (Kingston); Oleksandr Lysenko, p. 10 (American crocodile); epantha/ Getty Images, p. 10 (fruit bat); Scubazoo/ Alamy Stock Photo, p. 10 (sea turtle); AGAMI Photo Agency/ Alamy Stock Photo, pp. 10 (woodpecker), 10-11; Sevenstock Studio, p. 12; Shahjehan, p. 13 (top); delaflow, p. 13 (bottom); Debbie Ann Powell, pp. 14, 15; Michael Ochs Archives/ Handout/ Getty Images, p. 16; Lost Mountain Studio, p. 17; MyLoupe/ Contributor/ Getty Images, p. 18; Monty Rakusen/ Getty Images, p. 19; picture alliance/ Contributor/ Getty Images, p. 20 (top); WENN Rights Ltd/ Alamy Stock Photo, p. 20 (bottom); Michael Dwyer/ Alamy Stock Photo, p. 21 (top); Ultimate Hero, p. 21 (bottom); Prisma by Dukas Presseagentur GmbH/ Alamy Stock Photo, p. 22; Paul_Brighton, p. 23 (ackee); from my point of view, p. 23 (jerk chicken); Rachael Barnes, p. 23 (grater cake); Jon Arnold Images Ltd/ Alamy Stock Photo, p. 24; Collin Reid/ AP, p. 25; Serjio73, p. 26; Aflo Co. Ltd./ Alamy Stock Photo, p. 27 (top); Mlpearc/ Wikimedia Commons, p. 27 (bottom); Glyn Thomas/ Alamy Stock Photo, p. 29 (dollar); Krzysztof Bubel, p. 29 (coin).